CULTS

TROUBLED

SOCIETY

CULTS

Renardo Barden

The Rourke Corporation, Inc.

The Rourke Corporation, Inc.
P.O. Box 3328, Vero Beach, FL 32964

Barden, Renardo.
    Cults / Renardo Barden.
        p. cm. — (Troubled society)
    Includes index.
    Summary: Discusses why and how religious cults begin and prosper, describes the different types, and examines in detail the events surrounding cult leaders Charles Manson and Jim Jones.
    ISBN 0-86593-070-8
    1. Cults—United States—Juvenile literature.   2. United States—Religion 1960-   —Juvenile literature.   [1. Cults.]   I. Title.
II. Series.
BL2525.B37   1990
302.3—dc20   90-41237
                                                                   CIP
                                                                    AC

Series Editor: Gregory Lee
Editors: Elizabeth Sirimarco, Marguerite Aronowitz
Book design and production: The Creative Spark,
    Capistrano Beach, CA
Cover photograph: Andrew Martinez/Photo Researchers, Inc.

CULTS

Contents

ONE

WHAT IS A CULT?

He claimed to have visions from God, so he led his people far away from the evils of the world and into the mountains. Then, to back up his claim of divine guidance, he seemed to perform miracles. He said he received spiritual laws that his followers were required to honor. He began writing down his story in the hope it would become law. What was this cult leader's name?

Many people would be shocked to think that the life of a man who contributed so much to the Judaic, Christian, and Islamic religions could be compared to today's leaders of "cults." Nevertheless, the biblical Moses who led his followers out of Egypt, parted the Red Sea, received the Ten Commandments, and wrote part of the Old Testament, was the ultimate cult leader.

Some people might object to this description. Yet all of the world's major religions once had the characteristics of cults. In any case, members of the groups discussed in this book would not want to be considered members of cults. Dislike of the word cult stems from the knowledge that it is often used to make small religious groups seem stranger and more harmful than they really are.

The followers of Jesus founded Christianity. Mohammed began the Islamic religion. Buddha became the central figure in Buddhism. And the sayings of Confucius became the basis of Confucianism. People too quick to use the word "cult" need to be reminded that Jesus, Mohammed, Buddha, Confucius and Moses were leaders of the most successful cults in the history of the world.

In fact, Jesus Christ was crucified for being a cult leader. The development of the Christian religion after Christ's crucifixion is the story of how a cult evolved into a

All the world's major religions were cults at one time—threats to the "normal" society of their day. Christianity began as a challenge to the Roman Empire, and blossomed into the world's largest religion.

major world religion.

Unfortunately, people tend to use the term cult carelessly, often to signal their refusal to respect the beliefs or leaders of other people or cultures. Too often the word is used to brand those who hold different values as sinners, heretics, or fools.

Cultus is a Latin word meaning "to cultivate" or to "till" or "plant." In gardens, seeds are planted, soil is tended, and something grows. What grows, of course, depends on what is planted. In the case of cults, what is "planted" are basic human desires—especially the desire to love and be loved by a community of human beings—and the desire to find a loving, higher power, usually thought of as God.

As we use it today, the word cult is what we call a "loaded" term. Loaded words are those which carry messages, often of contempt. When any elderly woman is called a "hag," or a homeless man a "bum," such names are derogatory and their use demonstrates prejudice, ignorance and dislike. Just as those words show contempt for men and women, so the use of the term "cult" often conceals the user's wish to condemn a religious group for intolerant reasons.

It is important that we remain aware of the attitudes and beliefs of religious groups, and that we observe not only what a group says it believes, but what it does.

Labeling a group a cult has often made the term meaningless because the word is being used carelessly. Its meaning can be made more clear if we use it carefully. *Webster's Dictionary* defines a cult as, "a system of religious worship or ritual." In this book, we will use the word "cult" to mean groups who believe that God or some other supernatural authority gives them the right to deny other people their basic civil rights, including the right to leave the group of their own free will at any time.

To use the word cult in this way is tricky since many religions, self-realization clubs and other organizations often share some—but not all of—the characteristics of a cult.

Cult Traits

Although authorities differ on some details, most

lists of cult characteristics include the following:

- An intensity and a certainty of belief
- A single strong and powerful leader
- A tendency to control communication
- A fund-raising and recruiting department
- A *hierarchical* organization; that is, a group with a tendency to be run by one leader and people favored by that leader
- A *totalistic* outlook; that is, a view that spiritual life in the group must be present 24 hours a day, and therefore allows members no time for other interests, work or hobbies.

Some or all of these characteristics also apply to churches, synagogues and other religious groups not ordinarily considered to be cults. The second and the last characteristics, however, are typical of most groups considered to be cults. Before we can understand strong leaders, however, we must learn to distinguish between authority and leadership.

Authority And Leadership

Put in the simplest possible terms, the world is organized around the need for getting things done. It takes more people to do things that need doing than it takes to describe or organize them. Thus, there are leaders and there are followers, with many more followers than leaders.

There are two kinds of leaders: policy makers and dictators.

Policy makers create and describe effective ways of getting work accomplished and planning how it will be carried out. Sometimes these policy creators are not readily visible, however, and the real leaders are the men and women whose job it is to persuade followers to carry out the policies.

For example, schools are usually run according to policies set by a school board. Each school has a principal who hires and oversees teachers to carry out the board's educational policies of teaching. Teachers exert leadership by persuading students to learn. Lesser leadership roles are filled by students themselves: the football captain, the student body president, the pretty girl who gets straight As, and so on. In this way, education policy travels from school board to principal to teachers to student leaders and parents (who encourage their children to learn). The followers of the policy are the students who are supposed to get a good education.

But while the school board and principal will agree that the school should teach English, your teacher might refuse. He or she could let it be known that from now on the students were going to watch music videos instead of study English. For this the teacher certainly would be challenged by the principal and the school board. Most likely, of course, the teacher would be fired.

But suppose—a little fantastically—that the teacher's refusal to teach English became a general rebellion. Suppose students said that unless music videos were allowed to replace English, they would stop attending school. Suppose the teacher was joined by other teachers who were weary of correcting English papers.

Backed by students and other teachers, the English teacher would then be able to force other

The satanic symbols and phrases spray-painted on this fence in Modesto, California, were explained as cult activity. Cults that claim to worship the devil frighten traditional religious groups, and this type of vandalism is of concern to law enforcement.

changes. As more and more people joined the teacher, the school board would become less and less important. In such a case, the teacher might well rise from a position of leadership to a position of absolute authority. With the backing of the students, he or she would be able to get rid of teachers and school board members they didn't like. In time, school authority would be in the hands of the teacher, who would then become a dictator.

Freedom Of Religion, Even For Cults

The first clause of the First Amendment to the United States Constitution reads:

"Congress shall make no law respecting an establishment of religion, or prohibiting the free exercise thereof..."

For more than 200 years the courts of our country have repeatedly ruled on a strict, literal interpretation of this amendment. It is significant that the men who wrote the Constitution felt this should be the very first item in the Bill of Rights. The word "cult" does not appear in the Constitution.

All people, whether natives of America or naturalized citizens from other countries, have the right to worship—or not worship—in any way they want to, without fear of repression. The First Amendment says a government cannot take away this human right. This type of religious freedom was generally unheard of before the establishment of the United States. And the United States has yet to experience any of the tragic, generations-old religious violence that marks the lives of people in such places as Northern Ireland and the Middle East.

Historically, most dictators come to have more and more power until eventually, other leaders arise to contain, limit, and diminish the dictator's power. The leader is then overthrown, and—in our fantasy—a new system for running the school would have to be created.

Dictators

Whether it is wielded by leaders or by policy, authority in a society exists because of agreements that are more broadly based and more enduring than individual leaders. Sometimes authority has human representatives in the form of kings, prophets, or presidents. Authority can also exist in a more abstract sense—as in a document like the Bible or the United States Constitution.

However abstract, authority can be challenged and weakened by strong leaders whose job it is to use their authority, but who instead abuse their authority. This means that respected individuals such as prophets, police, lawyers and religious leaders and politicians are important to human social order, but they can also be potentially dangerous to human freedom. Under conditions of social unrest, people hunger for strong leaders. This is often the reason why a strong but corrupt leader is placed in a position of power.

TWO

Cults Of Personality

Organizations that many people think of as cults often grow strong when there are people who have social, psychological and spiritual needs that are not being met by policy makers and other local leaders. These organizations can be religiously, militarily, or even criminally oriented. To be effective, a leader must persuade his or her followers that they know the problems and issues of the day better than anyone else. Such a cult is a *cult of personality.*

This was the case with the cult killer Charlie Manson, who fulfilled several young women's desires to belong, share drugs and racial fears, and have a leader who would assume absolute control over their lives. He persuaded them that he knew what they needed in order to have a better life. Manson provided them with love, punishment, and approval. In exchange, they obeyed him. They even killed for him.

This same hunger was also true—on a much larger scale—with Adolf Hitler, the Austrian army corporal who came to power in Germany in 1932. After gaining popularity and the following of hundreds of thousands of people, he led Germany into World War II in 1940.

The Nazi Era

In the 1930s, the German people were unhappy with the Treaty of Versailles, the agreement of 1919 that ended World War I. The treaty had demanded much from the country that lost, and the Germans were suffering great economic hardships. Many blindly blamed the Jews for their troubles. Hitler knew how to present himself as a hero and a martyr to popular ideas. His book, *Mein Kampf* ("My Struggle"), written while he was in prison,

The Nazi movement of Adolf Hitler was a cult of personality, where an entire population surrendered their power to a single, powerful leader. This cult lives on among a tiny minority of Americans who belong to the American Nazi party.

became a cult book. His philosophy helped Hitler fan the flames of anti-Semitism or anti-Jewish feeling in Europe.

Hitler was a highly excitable and hypnotic speaker. With shouting and tearful speeches, he persuaded most German people that he not only felt the injustices of Germany more keenly than anyone else, but that he knew what to do about it. He promised to restore Germany to the position of world power. In time, the ideas of the original Nazi Party, of which Hitler fast became the leader, were sacrificed to the emotional appeal of Hitler and his sermons of hate. The Nazi Party became a Hitler cult, and the German government eventually became a cult of personality. Hitler was known as *der Fuhrer* ("the Leader"), and ruled Germany by whim.

In 1945, when it became clear that the Germans would be defeated, Hitler and a small group of followers retreated into a state of religious fantasy involving Teutonic knights, the German soul, the music of Richard Wagner, astrology and vegetarianism. Rather than spare the people and land he supposedly loved and understood, Hitler allowed the Allied Powers to virtually destroy Germany before committing suicide.

The life and death of Hitler reflect what some experts say is a tendency for leaders whose policies are failing to enter into a false world of personal spirituality and fantasy. Hitler, for instance, became more concerned about his diet and his dog than his bombed cities and starving troops.

Ironically, even during times of tremendous upheaval, when government bureaucracies are frustrated by their efforts to carry out policy, a leader can emerge. In such crises, these charismatic leaders have a way of becoming more important than usual.

Hitler was a world leader as well as a cult leader. So too was Joseph Stalin, the murderous dictator of the Soviet Union both before and after World War II. Other leaders with enormous influence during that era were Benito Mussolini of Italy, Winston Churchill of England, Francisco Franco of Spain, and Franklin D. Roosevelt of the United States.

Spiritual Politicians

There were two cult figures from the World War II era that seemed to straddle both religion and politics. They seem to bridge the gap between the personality cults that dominated world politics in the 1940s, and the spiritual cults that came to prominence in the 1970s.

Japanese militarists who began the war with the United States by bombing Pearl Harbor in 1941 refused to make peace, even after Japan had been nearly destroyed by American bombing. Japanese Emperor Hirohito, who was a deity to his people, finally persuaded the Japanese that surrender was best. In so doing, he changed Japanese history. Never before had the Japanese emperor become involved in worldly affairs. As a condition of surrender, Hirohito was obliged to tell the Japanese that he was not a god.

Mohandas Gandhi was another international figure whose leadership had both spiritual and worldly implications. His doctrine of *Satyagraha*—or passive resistance—called for a polite refusal to cooperate with the British, who ruled India in the early 20th century. Because of the essential goodness of his policy of non-resistance, Gandhi was able to win an immense following all over the world. In time, through his efforts, India was granted independence from England. Gandhi's ideas were put to use in the United States in the 1960s by civil rights leader Dr. Martin Luther King, Jr., among others.

Only a few strong leaders who wielded enormous power with their personalities emerged after the 1940s. Mao Zedong was one, ruling the People's Republic of China with a doctrine named after him—Maoism. Several other dictators have had long reigns, including Fidel Castro of Cuba and Juan Peron of Argentina. But their followers generally lacked the unquestioning loyalty that gave someone like Hitler such power. For the most part authority in our time has rested more with government bureaucracies than individual leaders.

Some experts believe that magnetic politicians will never again be able to enjoy the complete and fanatical support of their countrymen because of modern technology. Instant communication in the form of satellite television networks with outlets in even the poorest nations make it hard to conceal the truth about other lands and other ways of life. Some people even wonder if the age of nationalism—keeping people separate behind national borders—is coming to an end.

The one recent exception to the disappearance of the cult politician has been the late Ayatollah Khomeini, former head of Iran, who came to power in 1979 and commanded absolute devotion from his countrymen. Khomeini's life is a particularly intriguing study in the way cult leaders become involved in political matters. He was one of the few leaders of modern times whose political power was considered to be based on his spirituality.

Many Moslems from Iran and other countries believed that Khomeini was a holy man and a leader of great importance. Christians in the United States and elsewhere, however, thought Khomeini was a fanatic who encouraged bloodshed in the name of his version of religious truth.

Indeed, until he died in 1989, the United States government treated Khomeini as if he were the leader of a terrorist cult, and Iranians were his cult members. Khomeini's rise to and administration of power in Iran makes one thing clear: one person's religion can be another person's cult.

Portrait Of A Cold-Blooded Cult Leader

Charles Manson never knew his father, and his mother was an alcoholic who left her son's caretaking to others so she could drink. As a boy and young man, Manson was always in trouble with the law. He spent many of his early years in reform schools and prisons.

Manson's days as the most infamous cult leader of the 1960s began with his release from prison and a move to San Francisco. There, among the hippies in the Haight-Ashbury neighborhood, he experimented with the drug LSD, listened to mystical talk of the hippies, and read about Scientology, a self-realization group.

Many young people in America during the 1960s gathered in San Francisco, where "peace and love" were said to prevail. Hippies prided themselves on being accepting of all people. Manson soon learned how to talk like a hippie and pretended to be very wise.

Many of the newcomers to San Francisco were young and had never been far from home. Manson kept a sharp eye out for young women who looked sad or confused. He made friends with them. He sang them love songs he had written. Then he persuaded them that he could help them find their way out of confusion and lead meaningful lives if they would dedicate themselves to him and obey him in all things. In a short time he had persuaded several young

Charles Manson and his Family were a tiny cult until they were convicted in Los Angeles for the murders of seven persons. Manson's followers believed that Manson had special powers and obeyed him completely—even when he ordered them to kill for him.

women to behave like slaves and do whatever he asked.

When Manson had been in prison he had never been particularly charming. Men who knew him in jail said he was mild-mannered and would pout rather than get involved in violent disputes with inmates. But the many young women who fell for Manson found him very charming. They admired his dark eyes and aura of mystery. They saw themselves as weak and helpless and Manson as strong—as strong as a god. They also saw him as a source of "spiritual" guidance. They obeyed him when he began to order them around and behave like a strict father.

"Strong leaders are sought because people in general are basically dependent on others and want to have somebody else solve their problems," says Dr. Marc Gallanter, who has spent many years studying cult behavior.

The followers of Charles Manson wanted him to solve their problems and guide them in a confusing and hostile world. The late 1960s was a time of extreme tension between black and white Americans. Manson believed that there would be a race war that would bring death to most white people, but that he and his followers would survive. Once most people were dead, he believed he would become the ruler of the world.

In 1968, Manson moved his followers—now called "the Frigate Family"—to Los Angeles, where he hoped to launch a recording career for himself. Several members of the Family were trained to sing the songs Manson had written, and the Beach Boys even recorded one of his songs, titled "Cease to Exist."

Eventually Manson and his Family moved to an old ranch where Manson started a business of stealing cars from the streets of Los Angeles and hiding them on the ranch. There they were turned into dune buggies and sold to people to drive in the deserts of Southern California.

As time went on, Manson's ideas became more and more bizarre. For example, he explained to his followers that the Beatles song "Revolution 9" was a reference to the Bible's Book of Revelation. He claimed that the Beatles song "Blackbird" was about the coming race war. He also said that rich people were "pigs," and that they should be killed as a punishment for their materialism.

In keeping with this strange philosophy, Manson thought of a horrible way to make his Family demonstrate their obedience to him. He ordered four of his followers to break into a home in Los Angeles and kill everyone they found inside the house.

On August 9, 1969, Susan Atkins, 21, Charles Watson, 23, Patricia Krenwinkel, 22, and Linda Kasabian, 20, dressed themselves in black. Wearing Bowie knives and carrying guns, they sneaked into the house.

Manson had a grudge against the owner of the house, Terry Melcher. Melcher owned a record company and had refused to record one of Manson's songs. So Manson sent his followers into the house expecting they would kill Melcher, but Melcher no longer lived there.

A beautiful, young movie star named Sharon Tate was renting the house. At the time of the break-in, Sharon had four guests. The Manson gang found them all at home.

First, they murdered 18-year-old Stephen Parent, then they slaughtered Abigail Folger and Folger's boyfriend, Voityck Frokowski. After they killed hairstylist Jay Sebring, they murdered Sharon Tate. Tate was eight-and-one-half months pregnant, and she begged her killers to let her live and have her baby. But they showed her no mercy.

When the group later told Manson that they had "killed five little piggies," he scolded them for doing sloppy work. The next night he took six Family members to the home of a wealthy husband and wife named LaBianca. Manson tied the LaBiancas up and ordered three of his disciples to kill and rob them. Then Manson left the house.

Shortly after these murders, the Manson family fled to the remote desert area of Death Valley in Southern California. There the group led a savage life, taking drugs, stealing more cars, and threatening local prospectors with knives. In investigating local complaints, the California Highway Patrol discovered the vehicles that Manson and his followers had stolen. They were arrested and tied into the killings.

Awaiting trial on another murder, Family member Susan Atkins told her cellmate about Charles Manson and the Tate and LaBianca killings. In time, Atkins told police everything they needed to know to charge Manson, Atkins, Krenwinkel, Kasabian and Watson with the seven murders.

Although Manson himself did not kill anyone, he had ordered the deaths. Many thought he was more guilty of the murders than the people who actually participated in them.

Manson was a charismatic cult leader. He did not publish materials or organize his followers into a religious group, or send them out to recruit new followers. But over time, his leadership of the Family was more and more like that of a leader of a religious cult. His followers called Manson "God" and "Satan." They fasted for him, and tried to communicate with him via spiritual experiments while he was in jail.

It's not likely that Manson could have become a religious figure outside the 35 or so people who accepted him as their leader, but in many ways his life fit the pattern of a religious cult leader. Some experts argue that religions are organized to express the intense attraction people sometimes feel for a single, charismatic leader. In fact, all of the world's major religions began as the teachings of one man; progressed to personality cults based on the personalities of their founders; and gradually became religions.

Students of *comparative* religions (the study of all religions) and anthropologists have suggested that just as every religion is founded by a leader—whether Moses, Jesus Christ, Mohammed, Buddha or Krishna, so every religion begins as a cult.

However much truth may be contained in that radical idea, it is certainly typical of the modern cult in that it develops around the personality of one leader.

THREE

THE NIGHTMARE OF JONESTOWN

In 1965 the Reverend Jim Jones, an ordained Methodist minister, decided that the city of Indianapolis, Indiana—where he served on the Human Rights Commission—was too racist for his liberal views. Believing that it was essential for blacks and whites to learn to live together in brotherhood, Jones—a white man—moved to Ukiah, California.

In California, Jones gathered about 100 followers and formed a church open to all races. He claimed to be a faith healer and to work miracles, even pretending to heal people of cancerous tumors. He showed his believers chicken entrails and said that they were cancerous growths that sick people had coughed up in response to his prayers for them. Eventually, Jones even pretended to raise people from the dead. Once he became a convincing faith healer and miracle worker, Jones moved to San Francisco, where in 1971 he established the People's Temple.

Psychologists say that the authority of a spiritual or psychological leader is only as strong as that leader's connection to a still-higher source of authority. Thus, the Reverend Jones sought more and more to link his own leadership with the authority of God. He gradually began to blur the distinction between himself and God. Finally, he told his followers that he was God's sole representative on earth, and that no one could be "saved" without him.

Jones promoted racial harmony through his People's Temple. He not only said that African Americans and white Americans were equal, but he also operated his church on those principles. He encouraged his followers to become active in politics. Because of their political

The Rev. Jim Jones founded the People's Temple in Northern California, but later moved his followers to the South American country of Guyana.

work, his followers were credited with helping elect the late George Moscone as mayor of San Francisco in 1975. Jones was named to serve as chairman of the San Francisco City Housing Authority in 1976. At the height of his popularity, Jones spoke to as many as 5,000 people a night, and claimed to have as many as 20,000 members in his People's Temple.

But things were not as they seemed to be. Jones

was not honest. After a time, former members of the Temple began publishing reports saying that Jones was stealing money from his followers, that he was punishing them severely, and that he faked miracles and faith healings.

To keep from being exposed and ruined, Jones told his closest followers that it was necessary to move the People's Temple away from San Francisco to a place where the evils of the world would not hurt the group. With as many followers as he could persuade to join him, he moved to the country of Guyana in northeastern South America.

The People's Temple In The Jungle

Jones and his followers leased 42 acres from the local Guyana government. They hacked away the jungle 150 miles north of Georgetown and created Jonestown, a series of rough but clean communal log buildings where nearly 1,000 People's Temple members lived and worked together.

But the rumors of cruelty and abuse did not die when Jones left the United States. Instead, they grew worse. Once he was in Jonestown, he became more of a tyrant than ever before, and word came back to America that life in the jungle was hard and cruel. Some people even said that Jones was going insane.

Shortly before Thanksgiving in 1978, Congressman Leo Ryan, a Democrat from San Francisco, flew to see the Jonestown compound for himself. He took 18 other people with him, primarily journalists and photographers. Ryan and his group learned that Jim Jones' people did not have enough to eat, that they were denied sleep, beaten, and forced to attend four- and five-hour religious services. Ryan was shocked by the unhealthy conditions and the depressed and fearful people he saw.

Ryan and others spoke with many members of Jonestown, but some were afraid to talk. Others were angry with Ryan and the intruders, and predicted that the congressman would bring trouble to the community. Some told Ryan that they wanted to return to the United States but were afraid that Jones would not let them leave.

Jones was upset that Ryan had come to his community with journalists and photographers. When he was told that some people wanted to return to America, he became angry. He said he was afraid that those who left the community would "lie," and he worried that the defectors' lies would destroy Jonestown. But the truth was horrible enough. Things were very bad in Jonestown. There was no need to lie.

The situation grew tense. While one couple argued about whether to leave or stay, one of Jones' followers attacked the congressman with a knife. Ryan was only wounded, but finally realizing that he and those who wanted to leave were in danger, he hurriedly took his party and 16 People's Temple members to a nearby airstrip. Ryan was anxious to get out and planned to fly to the Guyanese capital of Georgetown in two planes that were waiting for him there.

But while the reporters and defectors were boarding the planes, one loyal Jonestown member pulled out a pistol and started shooting. Two people were wounded.

Then several of Jones' followers came running out of the jungle and attacked those trying to board the planes. Congressman Ryan, three journalists, and one 18-year-old Jonestown defector were shot and killed. Ten other defectors and journalists were wounded. One of the two planes was able to take off and fly to Georgetown to get help.

Meanwhile, Jim Jones was informed that Ryan and others had been killed. He immediately summoned more than 900 of his followers and had armed guards surround the compound.

Vats of poisoned Kool-Aid were brought out. Jones instructed his followers what to do. He told them they must obey. Parents were told to squirt Kool-Aid down the throats of their small children, then drink the poison themselves. Some adults did so of their own free will, while others refused. The armed guards forced everyone to drink. Then Jones, age 46, apparently shot and killed himself with a pistol. No one in Jonestown survived.

The next morning at dawn, Guayanese soldiers flew into Jonestown, where they found 911 corpses in the mud, including the body of Jim Jones. They also discovered $500,000 in cash, $500,000 in gold, 30 automatic weapons, and many uncashed Social Security checks that older Americans who lived in Jonestown had signed over to Jones.

San Francisco, home to Congressman Ryan and most of the People's Temple members, was grief-stricken. Some who belonged to the group but had stayed in America feared that they, too, would be killed by a few extremists who remained loyal to Jones. More than 200 San Franciscans were given bodyguards.

The entire world was shocked. People simply could not understand how so many people could kill themselves because of their religious beliefs. They also couldn't understand how so many could follow one abusive man to their death, and even kill their own children.

Reaction To The Killings

The first reaction of people trying to understand tragedies like the Manson killings or the Jonestown suicides is to look for an easy explanation, like the People's Temple was a *cult*, and Jim Jones was a *cult* leader. It was easier to blame Jones for the mass suicide at Jonestown than to ask why nearly a thousand people had dedicated their lives and deaths to him, went with him into the jungle, and drank poison.

Similarly, people found it easier to blame Charles Manson for the Tate and LaBianca murders than the young killers who did his bidding. Although Manson and Jones committed tragic crimes for which they must be held responsible, they were not *solely* responsible. Manson and Jones were made scapegoats, people blamed for evils greater than they could be responsible for by themselves. The others who willingly participated in these tragedies did so because they wanted to follow the orders of their leaders.

Certain religious leaders in the United States spoke out in a rage against Jim Jones and what happened at Jonestown. Many of these same religious leaders used the horror of Jonestown as a way of recruiting and encouraging followers into their own beliefs. Many relatives of the victims saw a chance to blame other people—or governments—for the misfortune of their own family members. A few people, who would come to be known as "deprogrammers," saw

The horror of mass suicide overwhelmed Guyanese officials who arrived at
Jonestown too late to save these people. More than 900 people were found dead
throughout the settlement. They had all died from drinking poison.

these tragedies as a chance to become heroes and
make money by rescuing victims of cult life.

People everywhere in America blamed the
Manson killings and the Jonestown massacre, along
with the disappearance of many middle-class
teenagers, on cults. Americans didn't always know just
what the new cults were about, or why people were
attracted to them, but they were getting tired of new
spiritual groups declaring they knew the truth about

life. In some other countries these groups might have been considered to be acceptable religions, but in the United States small, unfamiliar spiritual groups and churches were labeled cults. Many people who had never studied human behavior or religions other than their own became excited and said that these groups were capturing the hearts and minds of American young people through the use of "brainwashing." This word implied that so-called victims of cults were tricked rather than honestly convinced of their religious conversion. Many people overlooked the American idea of freedom of choice—especially in matters of religion.

A MYSTICAL DECADE

The generation of Americans born after World War II came of age in the 1960s. They did not suffer the economic hardships of the Great Depression, or endure the agonies and hardships of a world war. Their early years were more comfortable than those of earlier generations. It seemed that humankind would soon end war and poverty using science and technology, and even travel to the moon. The "baby boomers" were an idealistic generation who had high hopes for the future, but they were not—by and large—a particularly religious generation.

By the mid 1970s, there were more than 800 different denominations of the Christian church active in the United States. Yet many people believed that only a handful of these religious organizations ever did anything to apply their religious values outside their own organizations. It also seemed to many that moral leadership in the world would not come from the Christian and Judaic religions. Many young people thought that established religions should have worked harder to stop the war in Vietnam or end racism. Instead, they were too caught up with potluck dinners, hymn singing, and denominational debates that did not matter in the real world. This generation was disillusioned, or cynical, about the values and beliefs of their parents and the "establishment."

When political activism began to taper off at the end of the 1960s, many young people hungered for spiritual values they felt no longer existed in traditional religious groups. They longed for a spirituality that encouraged them to challenge authority. They wanted a spiritual life based on accomplishment rather than on the appearance of virtue.

A former cult member named Robert Perez put it this way. "We read too much. We read too many books and we believed what they said. We read the Bible. We read all the great antiwar novels. Our parents never read them. I read them and I believed them. Martin Luther King, Mahatma Gandhi, the whole thing —I believed it. Brotherhood. I just couldn't relate to the fact that people have to shoot one another, or to nationalism and wars and racial tensions."

In those days, a Harvard professor named Timothy Leary and other psychologists began experimenting with the drug LSD. They said LSD made it possible for people to become more "conscious" of the world around them. LSD, peyote, and other so-called mind-expanding drugs attracted the interest of the Beatles, Bob Dylan, and other popular figures of that generation. People spoke of achieving a higher consciousness that could lead to a world saved by peace and love.

Although some people took drugs out of boredom or for pleasure, many took them in search of spiritual knowledge. Many decided later that they didn't need drugs to achieve a higher consciousness, and instead they took an interest in ideas and religions that studied human consciousness and spirituality through *meditation*. Meditation means quietly controlling one's breathing while concentrating on one idea, one word, or one object—or sometimes, nothing at all. This is supposed to help the meditator achieve "harmony." Spiritual ideas such as this became popular. They originated in India, China, Japan, and Native American cultures, and they seemed all the more significant because they were foreign and mysterious. More and

Maharishi Mehesh Yogi, an Indian guru, lectured a great deal in the United States throughout the late 1960s and 1970s. His Transcendental Meditation movement was a very popular Eastern-influenced religion at that time.

more people of this generation searched for a spirituality that emphasized feeling over learning, and knowledge over faith.

Some (but not all) cult movements of the past 25 years had their roots in the desire of people who wanted to recreate the "high" they received from drugs with a spiritual high. These spiritual highs were difficult to gain without proper guidance and teachers—the kind

Western religions did not offer.

In 1965, when the Asian Exclusion Acts were repealed, many thousands of Asian people who had once been excluded from the United States because of the racist fears of earlier generations were allowed in. Some Asians who moved to America were true spiritual teachers while others, seeing the interest of young people in Asian philosophy, pretended to be. A few returned to Asia and brought back more teachers or *gurus* to the States.

Thus most of the religious groups and cults that became popular in the late 1960s and early 1970s were the result of what one authority called "galloping Orientalism." In other words, the enthusiasm for Asian religions and religious leaders fit the spiritual hunger of the times.

Types Of Cults

Although spiritual groups and cults tend to be as individual as the people who start or join them, they also have many characteristics in common. For instance, experts generally agree that there are two types of cults: messianic and millenarian.

Messianic Cults. The word messianic comes from *Messiah* (Hebrew for "annoited one"), and a messianic cult is a group that places great reliance on the power and spirituality of its leader. Many sacrifices must be made by followers on behalf of the leader. In return, the leader is supposed to "save" his followers. Jim Jones and Charlie Manson led messianic cults.

Millenarian Cults. The word millenary comes from the Latin word for 1,000, and refers to the 1,000-year reign of Christ predicted in the Book of Reve-

Millenarian cults proclaim the end of the world, and often name the exact date of Armageddon (when Christ will return and judge the human race). Jehovah's Witnesses are often seen in public places displaying their literature, telling people that it's not too late to be saved.

lations in the Bible's New Testament. Generally speaking, millenarian cults are spiritual organizations that predict dramatic events that include some version of the end of the world. Manson predicted that there would be a race war, which he expected to bring about a changed world. So his family can be thought of as a cult with millenary characteristics.

Millenary characteristics can be shared by groups which are not necessarily cults. For instance, Jehovah's Witnesses are always predicting the end of the world. Other groups even specify the exact date and time when "Armaggedon" will end all life on earth. When a given date arrives and the world doesn't end, they simply change the date. The Church Universal and Triumphant, described later in this book, is also anticipating the end of the world. Millenarian groups and cults survive by changing the date of the anticipated ending or by saying that the ending has been postponed, often through prayer.

Another way to broadly define cults and groups is to classify them as Asian-Oriented, Christian-Oriented, and Scientific-Oriented.

Asian-Oriented Cults. Asian religions were popularized in 1965 after the repeal of the Asian Exclusion Acts. Some examples:

- A man named Prabhupada arrived in 1961 to start the International Society for Krishna Consciousness.
- In 1971, a 13-year-old guru called Maharaj Ji arrived in America and started the Divine Light Mission.
- In 1981, Bhagwan Rajneesh arrived from Poona, India, and moved to Antelope, Oregon, where he settled it with Rajneeshees.
- Perhaps most successful of all was the Transcendental Meditation Society, a group headed by Maharishi Mehesh Yogi. It emphasized meditation, and even succeeded—for a time—in getting it taught in some American school classrooms.

Christian-Oriented Groups. Not every young person in America adopted Asian philosophies and ideas. Some, particularly those with strong early ties to evangelical Christian religions, were drawn to extreme or variant forms of the Christian faith.

- Chief among these was the Unification Church of Sun Myung Moon, which taught that Moon himself was the successor to Jesus Christ. Moon arranged mass marriages for his followers and became the best known target of anti-cult groups.

- Also of wide and controversial interest was the Family of Love or Children of God, founded by David Berg, who came to call himself Moses. Berg made his female disciples have sex with potential converts.

Scientific-Oriented Groups. Some groups avoided both Asian and Christian ideas in order to impart a psychological or scientific legitimacy to their spiritual quest. For the most part, these groups tend to be less cultish, if only because they addressed the mind.

- Chief among these is the Church of Scientology, founded by L. Ron Hubbard in the 1950s and dubbed a religion primarily for tax purposes and constitutional protections. Through the use of an "E-meter," an electronic device similar in kind to "lie detector" polygraph machines, Scientologists "free" the mind of "engrams" or psychic wounds.

- Another scientific cult is the arm of the Transcendental Meditation Society, called the World Plan Executive Council, which attempted to establish scientific proof of the benefit of transcendental meditation and encouraged scientific research on a variety of its claims for spirituality.

Hare Krishna

Among the first gurus who arrived in the 1960s was an old man from the country of India who became known as Prabhupada (Prob-hu-pa-duh). In 1965 he founded the the International Society for Krishna Consciousness (ISKON) in New York. He instructed followers that if they wanted a spiritual life they should chant the name of *Krishna*, a Hindu god who granted powerful spiritual states or "God-consciousness" on those who honored him.

Prabhupada encouraged his followers to do as religious seekers in India had done for hundreds of years—to beg for the money needed to survive. Funds not needed for food and shelter went to publications and efforts to convert others to the group. Full members of ISKON shaved their heads, wore orange robes, practiced vegetarianism, and renounced private property and sex. Despite the group's strict rules, at one time the group claimed as many as 250,000 members all over the world.

When Prabhupada died in 1977, there was no one to take his place at the head of ISKON. But before he died, he chose eleven men from among his staunchest followers to cooperate and carry on the work. But they did not cooperate; instead they quarreled because each wanted to lead the movement himself.

Within only a few years after Prabhupada's death, the group was racked by rivalries and worse: charges of murder, child molestation and drug dealing. Today, less than 500 of the 4,000 members originally initiated by Prabhupada remain in the organization. Authorities say that now the group has fewer than 10,000 active members.

Many Americans who saw Krishna members on city streets, college campuses and in airports were offended by their shaved heads, begging and rudeness.

"Hare Krishna" is the chant of this well-known cult, in which members shave their heads, wear *saris* (an Indian garment) and beg for money.

Some objected to their beliefs, and still others criticized their behavior. Americans generally were annoyed that the Krishnas were allowed to ask for money, and refused to contribute. The Krishnas met this resistance not by giving up begging, but by shedding their orange robes, looking more conventional, and lying about who they were and what they would do with the money. They did not consider this wrong, rather they believed that whatever they did in the name of Krishna would be for the good of the human race.

That's one reason so many people object to groups like the Krishnas. They tend to believe that whatever they do in God's name will turn out all right. They think they can justifiably disregard laws and ordinary codes of moral behavior because they do it for their God. Other cults have often adopted similar attitudes. For example, high officials of the Church of Scientology were convicted and imprisoned on conspiracy and burglary charges in the 1970s. The Church was obsessed with learning what the federal government knew about Scientology.

Cults in the United States always want the constitutional protection offered a religion; however, they don't always protect the rights of their own members. And some groups seem interested not in the spiritual well being of their members, but rather in enriching their leaders.

Throughout history, many religious groups have justified violating civil law by citing a higher law, saying that God's ·interests are above the rules of men. Such people are said to believe that "the end justifies the means." In other words, if a goal is worthy enough, the misdeeds done to reach that goal can be forgiven.

Ironically, aggressive anti-cultists called "deprogrammers" practiced the same philosophy as the cults they were supposed to be fighting. In the name of "rescuing" American young people caught up in cults, deprogrammers decided that their end also justified the means. They justified their deception and kidnapping on the basis of what they call brainwashing.

A Cast Of Cults

Cults large and small come in many forms, appeal to a wide variety of ages and ethnic groups, and include widely diverse beliefs. Some cults persist for generations, while others fade into obscurity. Not all of them claim to be religions or churches. Here is just a sampling of cults that have appeared in the United States.

Eckankar. Founded in 1965 by Paul Twitchell (a former Scientologist), followers of this movement believe in soul travel, mind reading and reincarnation. Primarily associated with the "New Age" movement.

Freemasonry. Now a respected community organization with some 16,000 lodges in the United States, the Free and Accepted Masons was once a mysterious brotherhood of craftsman (masons are builders) having secret rituals, initiations and symbols. Many prominent men have been freemasons, including Benjamin Franklin and Wolfgang Mozart.

The Rosicrucian Society. Appearing first in 1623 in Paris, France, the "Rosy Cross" brotherhood promised those who joined that they would help the world achieve universal peace. The mysterious order was popular with certain European intellectuals, but remained obscure until a modern version was founded in the United States in the early 20th century. The headquarters are now in San Jose, California.

Church of Satan. Although "satanism" or devil worship is occasionally blamed for bizarre incidents in some American communities, the existence of any organized satanic church is poorly documented. There was a Church of Satan founded in 1967 that was supposedly based upon the writings of Aleister Crowley, an Englishman at the turn of the century, who claimed to worship the devil.

Church of Scientology. Founded in 1954 by the late L. Ron Hubbard, a science fiction author, Scientology claimed some three million members in the 1980s. Its headquarters are in Los Angeles. Scientology dwells on improving the human mind, clarifying communication, and purging negative emotions. Church members pay thousands of dollars for this "auditing" process, and advanced students learn that humans share the memories of alien souls that lived billions of years ago in other galaxies. The chief work describing Scientology is Hubbard's book *Dianetics*, which is still widely available.

The Theosophical Society. The name is taken from the Greek word *theosophia,* meaning "divine wisdom." The founder, a woman named H.P. Blavatsky, described the Society as "a philanthropic and scientific body for the propagation of the idea of brotherhood on practical instead of theoretical lines."

The Way International. Supposedly, God spoke to Victor P. Wierwille in 1942. By 1957, he had founded The Way to promote strict biblical interpretation as a guide to living. Among The Way's beliefs is that Jesus was not a Jew. Their symbol is not the Christian cross but a tree.

The World-Wide Church of God. Herbert W. Armstrong was an early radio and television evangelist who eventually founded his mission in Pasadena, California. This organization claims some 70,000 members, and declares that it is the "only true church."

FIVE

DEPROGRAMMING AND THE NEW AGE

The term "brainwashing" came into use in the early 1950s after America fought in the Korean War. Korean and Chinese Communist military personnel had practiced a very intense kind of psychological and physical torture when it came to questioning American prisoners of war.

For example, an American prisoner of war might be questioned for hours and hours by different interrogators with no chance to rest. He would be insulted, flattered, slapped, shouted at, and beaten. He would not be given enough to eat or drink, and would not have adequate sleep. In time, many prisoners broke down under this sort of treatment. They told their captors everything they knew, cried, laughed, promised to become a Communist, and sometimes even signed a paper denouncing the United States.

In theory, people who were "brainwashed" would do or say whatever their captors told them to do. Hollywood made a movie about this called *The Manchurian Candidate*, and Americans found the whole idea of brainwashing a human being very frightening.

The reality of it all, however, turned out to be less dramatic. Of hundreds of American soldiers subjected to this barbaric treatment in Korea, only a very few broke down completely, and fewer still signed a confession or statement blaming the United States for the war. Only four or five chose to stay in Korea, and some came home later.

So the idea of brainwashing of young people by cult leaders became a popular and frightening belief by

The Rev. Sun Myung Moon of Korea claimed to be the latest *messiah* or savior to appear on earth, and his many followers worshiped him as God's messenger. Many of the Moonies were sought by deprogramers hired to bring them "back to the real world."

many Americans. Parents of children who joined cults couldn't understand their children's behavior, and took drastic steps to get them back. They knew that living with a cult was totally different from their world.

In fact, one of the primary characteristics of cults and some religious groups is that they are *totalistic*. They require members to be attentive 24 hours a day. In many cases the members all live together in communes where food and work are shared, and where all members follow the rules laid down by the guru or teacher. Members of these groups are often told that if they hope to achieve spiritual happiness, they must give up the past, including all their worldly goods and all ties to their families.

This was when deprogrammers came on the scene. Deprogrammers were agents of force hired by parents to rescue their children. But what parents and deprogrammers called "rescue," the victims and cults called "kidnapping." There are laws against kidnapping in every state but, in many cases, these laws were ignored when it came to deprogramming. The sympathies of society tended to be with the parents, and against the cults and their young members. But while some said deprogramming was a good thing, others argued that young people should have a right to practice the religion of their choice, even if they were wrong.

Eventually, forced removal of members from cults turned into many lawsuits across the country. Parents and grown children sued one another. Congressmen introduced legislation that sought to control cults. But because one person's cult can be another person's religion, the results of these efforts were negative.

Ted Patrick, Deprogrammer

Ted Patrick was a 40-year-old high school dropout when he first came to national attention in the early 1970s. Patrick and a man named William Rambur organized a group of parents whose largely adult children had joined the Children of God cult. Patrick's group called itself the Parents' Committee to

Free Our Children from the Children of God, or FREE-COG.

In connection with FREE-COG, Patrick developed a method of what he called deprogramming. As practiced by Patrick and his supporters, the deprogramming involved kidnapping members of a religious group and subjecting them to intense psychological arguments to change their way of thinking. At first Patrick concentrated on deprogramming only Children of God members, but later, after being contacted by other worried parents, he kidnapped members of other groups as well.

Because some cults such as the Children of God truly did abuse their members, Ted Patrick was at first seen as something of a hero. But not all the groups were abusive and, in any case, their members had a right to become and remain members of religious groups of their own choosing.

Patrick usually worked with one or more assistants; and sometimes with the relatives of the member to be deprogrammed. They would stake out the cult commune or headquarters and watch for the member they wanted to separate from the group. They would catch the victim unaware, throw him or her into a car, and drive to where the member could be treated. These methods were similar to the ways in which the Communists treated American soldiers in Korea.

Patrick agreed his methods were harsh, but he said it was the only way to "rescue" cult members. Once the cult member had been isolated, scolded and insulted for days without sufficient rest, he or she usually gave in and said yes, the cult had brainwashed them. When this happened, the person was considered to be deprogrammed. Many escaped, however, and went back to their cults. At least one-half of these efforts to deprogram cult members failed.

In 1974, the National Council of Churches finally spoke out against Patrick and his deprogramming. The Church of Scientology, the controversial self-help group some people regard as a cult, publicized stories of members who had experienced deprogramming, then decided to resume their membership.

Many of the people who were snatched from their groups were grateful to Patrick, but others were outraged and sued both their parents and Patrick. Although the courts sometimes sided with the deprogrammers and the parents, at other times they sided with the victims. In time, Patrick had to give up deprogramming because he could no longer afford to be sued.

Eventually the excitement and anger about cults died down. Interest in exotic forms of religious salvation fell off in the 1980s, and thankfully there have been no more Jonestown suicides. But sex scandals, drug dealing and criminal activities continue to discredit existing cults. But aggressive "new age" religions or cults are still in business and actively seeking new members.

Three Cults For The 1990s

Cults of the 1960s and 1970s tended to be both mystical and religious. People joined them out of a sense of idealism. They believed that belonging to a cult might provide them with spiritual fulfillment and bring them closer to God or their own souls. Those cults tended to be national or international in scope, with tens or hundreds of thousands of members all over the world.

Cults of the 1990s, however, seem to be less religious and more specific in their aims and purposes. They generally have much smaller and more localized memberships, and seem less inclined to borrow from the ancient religions of Asia.

In October of 1988, an eight-year-old girl named Dayna Broussard was beaten to death in Clackamas, Oregon, by four adult members of the Ecclesia Athletic Association. They were supposedly "disciplining" Dayna for breaking one of the group's rules. The founder of the cult was the girl's father, Eldridge Broussard. But he was not present when his daughter was beaten to death.

The association was formed by Broussard as a branch of his Watts, California, church: the Watts Christian Center. Broussard created the commune in 1982, and brought about 50 children to Oregon from the African-American ghetto of Watts to train them for Olympic events. Broussard believed that he would show the world what discipline could do for a group of disadvantaged youth, and imagined that many of the youngsters would become Olympic athletes. He said their careers would help support Ecclesia. Broussard was not charged in his daughter's death, but four adult members of the association were sentenced to prison for the beating. The Ecclesia Athletic Association has since left Oregon.

Not many cults are led by women, but the Church Universal and Triumphant (CUT) is headed by Elizabeth Clare Prophet. She lives with close to 3,000 followers in Montana's Paradise Valley, where the

"Survivalists" are people who believe that society as we know it will end because of wars and natural disasters. They prepare themselves by learning how to use firearms, storing food and other necessities in secret locations, and studying how to live under harsh conditions. Some people believe this is cult-like behavior.

group has constructed 46 underground shelters on a 30,000-acre ranch. While much of the world now feels safer from the threat of nuclear war than at anytime since the 1960s, Prophet's followers have stockpiled their shelters with food and supplies because she insists that nuclear war is at hand.

Prophet's spiritual beliefs are as exotic as her ranch. She believes that Jesus, Pope John XXIII,

Confucius, Christian saints and angels all speak to the world through her. She says she also communicates with Buddha, Shakespeare, Merlin the magician and Christopher Columbus. People from all over the country have recently arrived at the ranch because Prophet told her followers that the world is going through a particularly dangerous time. If there is no nuclear war, though, Prophet's religious group will not necessarily break up. She believes that if the world is not destroyed it is because the prayers of CUT have been heard, and that the world has been granted mercy.

Certainly one of the oddest groups to surface in a long time is the Eternal Values organization of New York City created by former male model Frederick von Mierers. He says that he comes from a star called Arcturus, and that he is the reincarnation of the Biblical prophet Jeremiah. His group is very small, elite and wealthy. It consists mainly of successful young models, mostly female, who buy gems and jewelry from him to protect their health and insure their powers. His gospel is a mix of jewelry, Eastern philosophy with his own twist, and cash. He sells cassettes and videotapes of his talks and gives "life readings" where he tells clients about their past lives for $350. At one time the group had about 100 people. Now it is down to about 50. Von Mierers is currently being investigated by the Manhattan district attorney's office.

SIX

SOCIETY AND RELIGIOUS NEED

Many settlers of the 13 original American colonies were people determined to practice various religions that were unacceptable in Europe at that time. Considering our origins, the importance of freedom of religion in America can hardly be exaggerated.

Not too long ago, Mormonism, Seventh Day Adventism and Christian Science (to name just three popular religious groups today) were widely considered to be cults. Now they have millions of believers in the United States alone, a good example of why we should not be in a hurry to judge a religious group to be a "cult."

We belong to a society that guarantees each of us the freedom to practice any religion we choose, or to ignore the claims made by religions. Americans are free to follow any religion that does not plot to overthrow the government or—as a matter of religious doctrine—commit crimes. The Constitution is quite specific in these guarantees. It also severely limits the rights of government or individuals to interfere in the private lives of its citizens.

But the Constitution does not and cannot protect American citizens from themselves. For example, no law can prevent Americans from surrendering their freedoms to a religious teacher who will tell them what to do and when and how to do it. Sometimes this creates a dilemma—an unpleasant choice.

American society is faced with the problem of preserving the rights of individuals and groups to worship and think as they please, while at the same time protecting the rights of citizens. Unfortunately, not all religious groups have democratic ideals. Some appear to be organized largely to enrich the people who created them or

Hate Thy Brother

A disturbing variation of cult behavior can be found in certain American groups obsessed with "racial purity," notably the Ku Klux Klan and the white "Aryan" groups. "Skinheads"—mostly young people who keep their heads closely shaved—often say that "Hitler was right," and that all peoples of color are inferior to whites. Anti-semitism (hatred of Jewish people) is also a repeated message of these groups.

The original Klan members came up with wild names for their officers such as Grand Wizard, Grand Dragon, Hydras — all mythical names. The idea of wearing white sheets was originally to scare blacks into thinking Klan members were ghosts. When the Klan changed their philosophy from just frightening blacks to murdering them, Congress investigated. In 1871 laws were passed to protect blacks' civil rights.

The Klan spread rapidly throughout the southern part of the United States, but membership was never constant, and many different "orders" branched off so there was no united Klan or single leader. As the Klan spread out, it weakened.

In the 1950s, however, the Klan made an ugly comeback when African-Americans began to campaign for civil rights. The Klan burned crosses near the homes of black people as a symbol of terror. Many black people were shot, hanged, or just disappeared as the Klan fought against the civil rights movement. A Birmingham, Alabama church was bombed and four black girls died.

The Klan claimed to be Christian, basing its philosophy of "white supremacy" on a vague mixture of the Bible and just plain bigotry. The kind of loyalty that Klan members demonstrate is very similar to the behavior of many cult followers, where there frequently is an "us" and "them" attitude. Their philosophy is simple: "They," the groups that are feared and hated, are always the source of society's problems. "Us" are always the good guys.

make the organizers famous. In fact, it seems that sometimes these groups seek the protection of the American legal system while denying basic rights to their own members.

The law in the United States says that an accused person is innocent of any crime until proven guilty. So should we hold that any group with expressed spiritual goals is a valid religion until it violates the rights of its members and otherwise earns the description of a cult? But if we do that, what is to prevent more Jonestowns? Should we try to prevent another Jonestown by making some religions illegal?

What we are really asking ourselves are questions about our constitutional freedoms. For example, should teenagers who are too young to vote be considered old enough to exercise freedom of religion? How old does a young person have to be to enjoy this constitutional guarantee? Or, if teenagers aren't allowed to choose their own religion, do they have the right to reject the religion of their parents? After all, is religious belief really sincere if it's forced on someone?

Should society do anything about adult Americans who sell their houses, give all their money to religious leaders, and—like children—place themselves under the total control of those leaders?

Is it okay to kidnap people from such groups, take them away, and try to talk them into abandoning their chosen religion?

The answer is that no, we cannot—not by law. The future freedom of our country depends on our willingness to be fair with all people, no matter how weak or misguided we think they may be. There are limits to what we can do to help or persuade one another to do what *we* feel is in *their* best interest. In fact, there are many reasons to believe that the American way of life depends on defining those limits, then learning to observe them.

Nobody can say what the future will bring, although it most likely will bring us more of the past, just in a different form.

America was founded in part by men and women seeking religious freedom that was tolerated nowhere else. Our Constitution was written by men who did not want to see religion dominate national life. The Constitution has been useful in keeping religious fervor from assuming a role in our national government.

Thanks to the Constitution, religious freedoms have been preserved here. And thanks to the American temperament, religious diversity has become a part of the American way of life. To echo an old campaign slogan, a chicken in every pot, a car in every garage and, for each man and woman, the religious freedom to worship as they see fit.

By practicing toleration and being patient with others' beliefs, we can preserve the separation of church and state that our forefathers thought so important. We might also learn something. And who knows? We might also make the world yet safe for freedom, peace and love.

Glossary

BRAINWASHING. The practice of radically changing a person's personality or beliefs against their will. Like hypnotism, brainwashing has never been shown to be completely effective in altering a person's behavior.

COMMUNES. Usually, a small group of people living together and sharing work, earnings, etc.

COMPARATIVE RELIGIONS. A program of study of all mankind's religious beliefs and practices, how they originated, and how they compare.

DEPROGRAMMING. The largely abandoned practice of kidnapping cult members in order to undo the alleged effects of brainwashing. Deprogramming techniques often resembled the methods of indoctrinating cult members in the first place.

HIERARCHICAL. A group of persons or things arranged in order of rank, grade, class, etc. A hierarchical cult is ranked by a leader, then trusted initiates or disciples, and then the followers.

MEDITATION. As a religious practice, one meditates by thinking of a single subject in one's mind, over and over, to achieve "peace" or higher "consciousness."

MESSIANIC CULT. A cult devoted to a single spiritual
leader who comes to rescue people on earth.

MILLENARIAN CULT. A cult that expects tremendous
change—even the end of the world—at the end
of 1,000 years (a millenium).

NAZISM. A 1930s political movement in Germany that
led to the rise of dictator Adolf Hitler. The Nazi
movement began World War II, and millions of
Jews, Russians and other Europeans were killed
because of racial hatred.

NEW AGE. A news media label for a whole list of sub-
jects and movements: interest in Eastern
religions, astrology and numerology, soul travel,
reincarnation, etc.

SAVED. Used to describe someone who accepts a
religious movement as the only truth about God
and/or the universe; "born again."

TOTALISTIC. Cults that require a round-the-clock
devotion to their religious practices. Members
and the goals of its leadership are totalistic.

Bibliography

Ancient Wisdom and Secret Sects. Time-Life Books, Alexandria, VA, 1989

Appel, Willa. *Cults in America: Programmed for Paradise* Holt, Rinehart and Winston, New York, 1983

Barker, Eileen. *The Making of a Moonie.* Basil Blackwell, Inc., London, 1984

Bromley, David G. and Phillip E. Hammond, Eds. *The Future of the New Religious Movements.* Mercer University Press, 1987

Davis, Deborah. *The Children of God.* Zondervan Publishing, Grand Rapids, MI, 1984

Enroth, Ronald M. *Youth, Brainwashing and the Extremist Cults.* Zondervan Publishing, Grand Rapids, MI, 1977

Enroth, Ronald and Others. *A Guide to Cults and New Religions.* InterVarsity Press, Downers Grove, IL, 1983

Hubner, John and Lindsey Gruson. *Monkey on a Stick: Murder, Madness and the Hare Krishnas.* Harcourt Brace Jovanovich, NY, 1988

Pavlos, Andrew J. *The Cult Experience.* Greenwood Press, Westport, CT, 1982